RACISM

by Emilie Dufresne

![BookLife PUBLISHING]

©2018
BookLife Publishing
King's Lynn
Norfolk PE30 4LS

All rights reserved.
Printed in Malaysia.

A catalogue record for this
book is available from the
British Library.

ISBN: 978-1-78637-428-8

Written by:
Emilie Dufresne

Edited by:
Robin Twiddy

Designed by:
Jasmine Pointer

PHOTO CREDITS

Front cover – Hogan Imaging, John Gomez, GagliardiImages. 2 – John Gomez. 3 – Hogan Imaging, GagliardiImages. 4 & 5 – qvist, Michael Dechev, Dmitri Ma, pixinoo, Bloomicon, Daniel Krason. 6 – M-SUR, nw10photography, Gustavo Frazao, FMStox. 7 – YAKOBCHUK VIACHESLAV, Aleutie. 8 – Kzenon, Brian A Jackson. 9 – GagliardiImages, Leigh Prather, kuroksta, ShendArt. 10 – SpeedKingz, Sandor Szmutko. 11 – dotshock, Dean Drobot, LineTale, Blan-k. 12 – wavebreakmedia, SpeedKingz, marysuperstudio, WindAwake. 13 – Dean Drobot, PR Image Factory. 14 – ChameleonsEye, Darren Baker, Diego Cervo, ShendArt. 15 – michaeljung, erlucho, vladwel. 16 – Monkey Business Images, Rawpixel.com. 17 – Sergey Novikov, GagliardiImages, Marina Solva. 18 & 19 – Elzbieta Sekowska, Alessia Pierdomenico, neftali, catwalker, 1000 Words, a katz. 20 – Lucky Business, Evan El-Amin, Sunflowerr. 21 – 1000 Words, Christopher Penler, Rvector. 22 – Rena Schild, ChameleonsEye. 23 – XiXinXing, Monkey Business Images, Sapann Design. 24 – Lopolo, Pressmaster. 25 – Monkey Business Images, Sergey Novikov, VikiVector. 26 – Janaka Dharmasena, ChameleonsEye, matrioshka. 27 – ChameleonsEye, M. W. Hunt. 28 – vladwel. 29 – DGLimages, Halfbottle, Alexandr III. Joseph Sohm, Review News, John Gomez, frikota.
Images are courtesy of Shutterstock.com. With thanks to Getty Images, Thinkstock Photo and iStockphoto.

CONTENTS

PAGE 4	**What Is Race?**
PAGE 6	**Discrimination and Prejudice**
PAGE 8	**What Is Racism?**
PAGE 10	**Why Are People Racist?**
PAGE 12	**Recognising Racism**
PAGE 14	**How Does Racism Make People Feel?**
PAGE 16	**How Can We Talk about Race?**
PAGE 18	**Racism in the Last Century**
PAGE 20	**Racism Today**
PAGE 22	**Things to Improve**
PAGE 24	**What Can We Do to Help?**
PAGE 26	**Case Study: Aboriginal People**
PAGE 28	**Activities**
PAGE 30	**Campaigns**
PAGE 31	**Glossary**
PAGE 32	**Index**

Words that look like **THIS** are explained in the glossary on page 31.

WHAT IS RACE?

Race can describe our skin colour and physical appearance, but it's more complicated than that. Human beings can be grouped in many different ways. For example, a person's nationality is how we group people based on the country they are from. A person from France would be French and a person from America would be American. Religion is another way in which people are grouped. Someone who follows the Islamic faith is a Muslim. But what about race?

Humans often group themselves by their race. In terms of our BIOLOGY, there is no difference between any of the races. We need to use other ways to describe and define them. The most obvious way to do this is through certain visible TRAITS, such as skin colour, facial features or hair type. But it's not quite that simple. Racial identity is very complex.

Your family HERITAGE can also be described as your race.

This map shows where a large part of the population IDENTIFIES their race as Slavic. Slavic people share a set of languages, cultural heritage and racial identity.

People might identify with a race that matches their PHYSICAL characteristics – for example, white, Black or Asian. Other people might identify with more than one race – if your parents have different races, you might identify as mixed-race, or biracial, as both races are a part of your racial identity.

Race can also mean belonging to a specific cultural or religious heritage, such as being Jewish. People of many nationalities in parts of Asia and Europe identify as being Slavic – so their nationalities might be Russian, Czech or American, but their racial identity would all be Slavic.

This family might think of themselves as both Jewish and Slavic. This means they are biracial.

DISCRIMINATION AND PREJUDICE

Racism is made up of a combination of both **PREJUDICE** beliefs and acts of **DISCRIMINATION**.

PREJUDICE

Prejudice is a belief, opinion or feeling that someone has towards a person or group of people. People who are prejudiced might believe that the whole of a group has a particular trait in common. This is called a stereotype. Some stereotypes can appear positive. For example, that people are good dancers because of the colour of their skin, or that certain people are very smart because of the country they were born in.

Even positive stereotypes are still prejudice.

DON'T MAKE ASSUMPTIONS

Some prejudices seem more negative. For example, that people smell because of the country they come from, or that some people are not very clever because of their hair colour. All stereotypes are harmful because they make you judge someone before you know them. Everyone is different regardless of their race, age or gender. You should get to know someone instead of stereotyping them.

6

DISCRIMINATION

Discrimination is when a person or group of people are treated unfairly because of their differences. It can take lots of different forms. Someone may discriminate against others based on age, class, gender and sexuality, as well as race.

Discrimination is when someone acts on their prejudiced beliefs.

Another form of discrimination is not including people in social activities based on their religion, race, sex or age.

EXAMPLE

There are lots of ways that people can discriminate. Imagine lots of different people have applied for a job and they all have the same skills. If the employer chooses one person over another because of his prejudices against certain groups, that is an act of discrimination.

Marino Bran...
Brainse Mari...
Tel: 833629

7

WHAT IS RACISM?

If you experience any racism, or see it happen to another person, it is important to report it to a responsible adult or the police.

Racism is a type of discrimination based on a person's race. Racism comes from the untrue belief that some races are better than other races. Racism can be expressed both as prejudice or discrimination. If someone believes something about one particular race, it is a prejudice. If someone acts differently or unfairly towards particular races it is an act of discrimination.

Acting on racist beliefs by verbally or physically attacking someone is known as a hate crime or hate speech and is illegal in some countries. Racist incidents can include bullying, verbal and physical abuse, threatening behaviour, online abuse or damage to property.

THE RACE RELATIONS ACT was made in 1965 in the UK, making racism illegal.

Some people might wrongly believe that one particular race is better than another because of social, cultural or INHERITED differences. Some people even believe that people from different races should not mix or have children together.

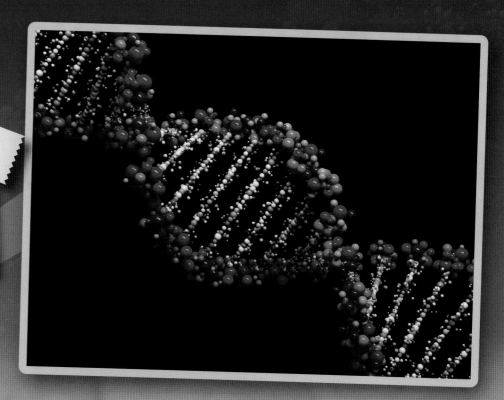

Every person should be able to live their life free from discrimination. Even though others may look or act differently from you, everybody should be treated equally. This is called equality.

Equality means that everyone gets the same treatment, rights and opportunities as everyone else.

WHY ARE PEOPLE RACIST?

As we grow up, our views, beliefs and even the type of language we use are influenced by people around us, for example our family and friends. If some members of a family hold prejudiced beliefs, these are often passed on to the younger people in the family.

This becomes a cycle. Prejudiced beliefs are passed on to the next generation and so on.

If others around us are using racist words or expressing racist beliefs, it may seem normal or acceptable because it is what we are used to. This does not make it right. It is important to stand up to racism.

Don't be afraid to question what someone says if you think they are being racist.

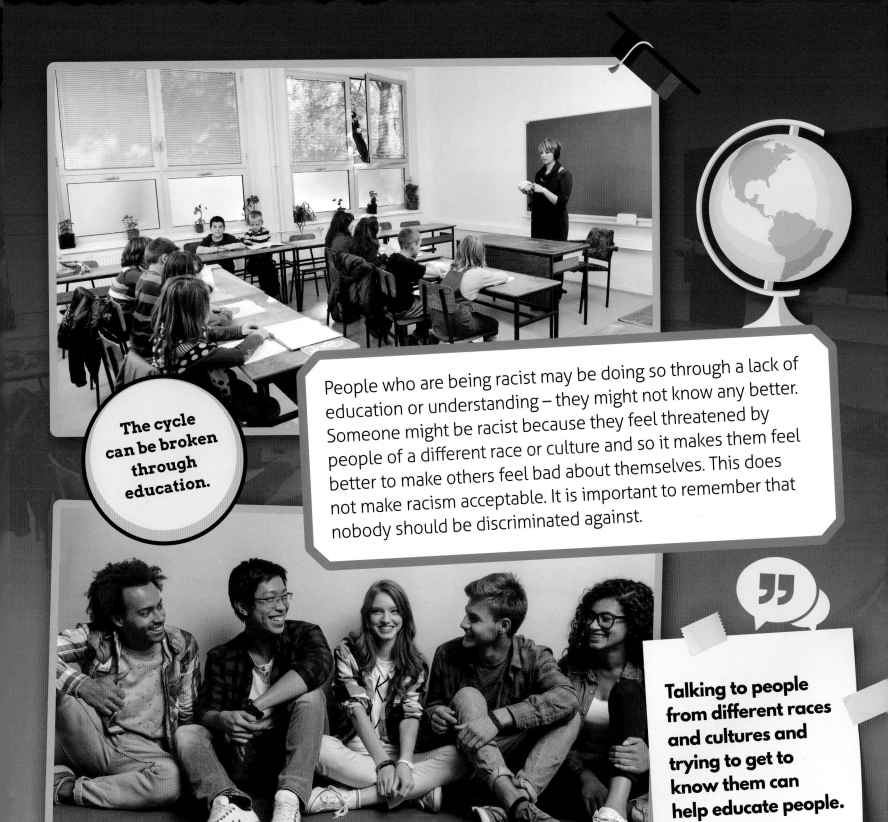

The cycle can be broken through education.

People who are being racist may be doing so through a lack of education or understanding – they might not know any better. Someone might be racist because they feel threatened by people of a different race or culture and so it makes them feel better to make others feel bad about themselves. This does not make racism acceptable. It is important to remember that nobody should be discriminated against.

Talking to people from different races and cultures and trying to get to know them can help educate people.

RECOGNISING RACISM

Racism can happen at any time and in any place. This includes at school, in public, at home and online.

This could be in the form of name-calling, physical abuse, or simply leaving someone out.

If a person is being bullied or singled out at school because of their race, this is racism. If you experience this, or see it happening to somebody else, it is important to report it to an adult or teacher that you trust.

CYBERBULLYING is any form of bullying that happens online. The most common platform for cyberbullying is on social media. If somebody online is using racist language, make sure you speak to a responsible adult about it.

Microaggressions are another form of racism. This is when a racist act or thought is carried out in a casual, and maybe unintentional, way. Because of this, some people might not even realise they are being racist when using a microaggression.

Can you help me with my maths homework?

Just because I'm Asian doesn't mean I'm good at maths.

Even though microaggressions aren't obviously mean, they can still hurt people's feelings. We must always think about what we are saying.

A question like this may seem harmless. However, it suggests that the person you are asking doesn't really belong in this country. This question comes from the assumption that someone is from somewhere other than the place they were born, based upon their race.

"But where are you really from?"

This is a microaggression.

HOW DOES RACISM MAKE OTHERS FEEL?

When a person experiences racism, they can feel lots of different emotions. These might include feeling sad, alone, angry or scared. For others, racist attacks can cause serious and long-term health issues, such as depression, anxiety or low **SELF-ESTEEM.**

A person experiencing racism might feel singled out. This could make that person feel lonely or as if they do not have anybody to support them. If you know somebody who might be feeling like this, it is important to let them know that they can talk to you or an adult about what is happening.

Even asking a simple question such as, "Is everything okay?" might let someone know you're there for them.

A person who experiences racism might feel it has affected their confidence. This could make that person not want to go to school or even leave the house.

Racist views that are passed down from parents and grandparents might make younger people feel that they can only be friends with certain people from certain backgrounds. It is important to make friends with everybody and make every person feel included.

Racism can create aggressive feelings inside a community. When a lot of tension builds up in a community it can lead to race related attacks and even RIOTS.

Protest!

HOW CAN WE TALK ABOUT RACE?

Sometimes it seems scary to ask someone about their race because we don't want to say the wrong thing and hurt someone's feelings. However, it can be useful to ask questions and understand more about certain topics related to race.

Everyone is different and that means that everyone will have different ideas about what they do and don't find acceptable. Just because one person from a certain race might be okay with something doesn't mean that everyone from that race or culture will feel the same.

QUESTIONS YOU COULD ASK

"WHAT RACE DO YOU IDENTIFY YOURSELF AS?"

"IS THERE ANYTHING THAT YOU FIND HURTFUL?"

"HAVE YOU HAD ANY RACIST EXPERIENCES?"

"HOW DID THAT MAKE YOU FEEL?"

"HOW ARE OUR BACKGROUNDS DIFFERENT?"

"WHAT FESTIVALS DO YOU CELEBRATE?"

"HOW ARE OUR CULTURES SIMILAR?"

"HOW DO YOU CELEBRATE THEM?"

Ciao

Hello

Hello

Hola

Привет

Bonjour

Hallo

You could also ask people from different backgrounds to tell you about their culture and lifestyle. This will help you both learn about different cultures, which will make them seem less scary.

When we ask questions like these, everyone becomes more educated about other cultures and races. It makes us realise that everyone is different in some ways and similar in others.. This helps us to break down stereotypes and prejudiced beliefs.

RACISM IN THE LAST CENTURY

1939 – WORLD WAR II BEGINS:
The Nazi party, led by Adolf Hitler, came to power in Germany in 1933. The Nazis believed they were a superior race and that others, particularly Jewish people, were inferior. During WWII the Nazis killed millions of Jewish people in one of the worst **GENOCIDES** in history.

1940s

1948 – APARTHEID IN SOUTH AFRICA ESTABLISHED:
Apartheid, meaning separateness, was a state of racial **SEGREGATION** in South Africa that was enforced by the country's government at the time. The government segregated all public services and services for white people were much better. People from different ethnic groups had limited rights. Apartheid ended in 1991, with the help of Nelson Mandela, who later became the president of South Africa.

1950s

1955 – ROSA PARKS:
Following years of racial segregation in America, Rosa Parks, an African-American woman, refused to give up her seat on the bus for a white person. This small act is largely thought to have begun the Civil Rights Movement, a movement that aimed to rid America of racial segregation.

Rosa Parks

18

1960s

1963 – MARTIN LUTHER KING JUNIOR: A leader in the Civil Rights Movement, Martin Luther King Jr. organised and led many non-violent protests against racial segregation. The most famous of these was the March on Washington. 250,000 people attended the march and it was here that he made his famous "I Have a Dream" speech.

1980s

Marino Branch
Brainse Marino
Tel: 8336297

1981 – BRIXTON RIOTS: The African-Caribbean population of Brixton, in South London, was suffering from high unemployment and crime rates. Relations between the community and the police were becoming increasingly tense, which eventually led to the uprising on the 11th of April. It is estimated that over 5,000 people were injured as a result. There have been several more riots in Brixton since.

1990s

1992 – LOS ANGELES RACE RIOTS:
The riots started in Los Angeles, California, and later spread to other areas of America. Riots began when four police officers were pardoned after a video of them beating Rodney King, an African-American, was shown in the media. The riots lasted for six days and over 2,000 people were injured. The army were eventually called in to stop the rioting, as local police forces failed to control the crowds of people.

19

RACISM TODAY

RACISM SINCE 2000

Since the year 2000, there have been many racist and race-related events across the globe. Although we have come a long way since the 1930s there is still a long way to go before we reach equality.

What good and bad things have happened since the year 2000 related to race?

In 2008, America elected their first Black president, Barack Obama. This was good for racial equality as it provided positive **REPRESENTATION** for Black people across America and the world. However, his presidency highlighted many racial differences in America that still need to be talked about.

In 2011, riots began across London. Much like the Brixton riots in the 1980s, these happened because of poor race-relations in London at the time. The riots were sparked when Mark Duggan, a Black man, was shot by police.

The riots started as a response to **POLICE BRUTALITY** towards **MINORITIES**, such as Black people, in the UK and America. Because the police had killed a Black man, people began to question whether the police treated white people better than racial minorities.

In 2017, the Charlottesville rally took place. It was organised by white **SUPREMACISTS**, and united all those in favour of racist beliefs and acts against minorities. Many anti-racism protests began against the supremacists. The rally highlighted how much racial unrest there still is in America.

THINGS TO IMPROVE

Although the world has made great progress with race relations in the last few decades, it is obvious that there are still lots of things that need to be improved. Some of these include **INSTITUTIONAL RACISM** and representation.

INSTITUTIONAL RACISM

Institutional racism is a form of racism that goes beyond an individual's beliefs. Instead, it refers to the collective failure of **ORGANISATIONS** to offer a service free from discrimination.

Both the media and the police are organisations that have been called institutionally racist. The media might only show certain races in its programmes, or show certain races in only negative ways. Some police officers might target groups of people based on their appearance, or stop certain people more than others because of how they look. These actions would be institutionally racist.

REPRESENTATION

Representation means that there is someone speaking on behalf of a group of people. Representation is a good thing if all different groups of people are represented. It is a bad thing if only certain groups are represented. People should be represented in lots of different areas such as on TV, in films, in schools and in discussions.

When America chose Barack Obama as their president, it was a big step for the representation of Black people in positions of power.

WHY IS REPRESENTATION SO IMPORTANT?

HAVING A VOICE

If people of all different races are represented in all different areas, it means that they have a position to talk about their beliefs and experiences. This helps promote equality and diversity.

ROLE MODELS

Representation is also important because it gives people ambition. If you see people of your race or culture in the leading role in an action film, as a headteacher, or in any position of power, this person becomes a positive role model. If you don't see people of your race and culture in these positions, it can make you feel alienated, or that you can't achieve the things that other races and cultures can.

WHAT CAN WE DO TO HELP?

CHANGE STARTS WITH YOU

There are lots of fun things you can do to promote equality and stop racism. However, it is important to remember that change starts with you! If you treat everyone equally and understand that everyone is different, it will help others do it too.

If you need help starting a conversation, look at pages 16 and 17.

TALK ABOUT IT

You could try to talk with people from different backgrounds to you, and see how they are similar and different to you. You should always think about what you say before you say it. If you hear someone saying something that you think is wrong you could tell them why it might hurt someone's feelings.

RAISE AWARENESS

Find out more on page 30!

You could go out of your way to make friends with people who look, speak and act differently to you. You could also raise awareness by inviting a charity to your school, such as Show Racism The Red Card, which runs educational days to teach people about equality.

HOLD A CHARITY FUNDRAISER

You could hold a charity fundraiser for a charity that aims to end racism. You could raise money by holding a bake sale, or a fancy dress day at school.

CASE STUDY: ABORIGINAL PEOPLE

The Australian Aboriginal people are INDIGENOUS to Australia. They have been living in Australia for over 50,000 years.

When the Aboriginal people first arrived in the country, and for many years after, they lived all over Australia. The Aborigines were mainly NOMADIC people who moved around looking for food; however, there were some who settled in one place. They created a rich culture, had many languages and had their own myths and legends.

Thousands of years ago, the different groups of Aboriginal people had over 250 languages. Now, there are fewer than 145 still known or used.

During the 18th century, people from Britain began to arrive in Australia. The British people used violence to claim much of the land, forcing the Aboriginal people to flee their homes. The British people wanted the Aborigines to join their culture and learn their language. However, the Aborigines resisted and this led to widespread fighting.

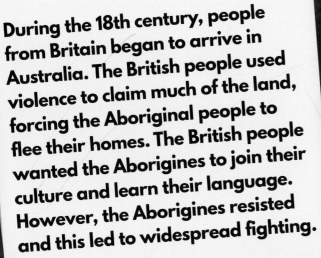

At this time, the attitude towards the Aboriginal people changed and they were forced out further. They were viewed as lesser than white people. The Aboriginal people still experience racial discrimination today and the community has suffered with poverty, high crime rates, a lack of jobs and poor education.

1. What is discrimination?

2. What is a stereotype?

3. What is racism?

4. What does the term "institutional racism" mean?

5. What is equality?

6. What is positive representation?

7. Name one charity that fights racism.

8. Name two ways that you can help stop racism happening.

9. Who made the famous "I Have a Dream…" speech at the March on Washington?

10. Who helped end apartheid in South Africa?

quiz

Answers:

1. Treating someone unfairly because of their differences.
2. A generalised belief about a whole group of people.
3. A type of discrimination based on someone's race.
4. Discrimination that comes from a whole organisation rather than an individual.
5. When everyone is treated the same.
6. When lots of different types of people are represented.
7. Black Lives Matter, Show Racism the Red Card, or Stand Up to Racism.
8. Hold a charity fundraiser and talk with people from different backgrounds to you.
9. Martin Luther King Jr.
10. Nelson Mandela

In small groups think about your favourite superheroes and book characters. Who are they? What colour skin do they have? What background do they come from?

Who has everybody else chosen? Do you notice any patterns? Are there lots of different people from different cultures and races? If yes, how are they different and how do they celebrate it? If no, why do you think this is?

A campaign is when a group of people work towards a goal by doing things such as organising events or putting up posters. Think about a possible campaign your class could start. Your campaign will need a slogan and an outline of your goals. Now create some eye-catching posters for your campaign.

A slogan is a short and memorable phrase used to get a message across.

29

CAMPAIGNS

SHOW RACISM THE RED CARD

There are many campaigns and organisations across the globe that aim to stop racism. Some of these include:

Show Racism the Red Card is a UK-based charity that promotes anti-racism by educating young people. The charity also uses footballers in short films that talk about issues surrounding racism.

BLACK LIVES MATTER

Black Lives Matter is an international organisation that aims to stop violence against Black people.

HTTP://WWW.THEREDCARD.ORG/

HTTPS://BLACKLIVESMATTER.COM/

STAND UP TO RACISM

Stand Up To Racism is a UK-based charity that stages demonstrations that aim to unite people from different backgrounds in the face of racism.

HTTP://WWW.STANDUPTORACISM.ORG.UK/

GLOSSARY

BIOLOGY	the science that studies the growth and life processes of living things
CYBERBULLYING	a form of bullying that is done online
DISCRIMINATION	the unjust treatment of people based on arbitrary reasons, such as their race, gender, sex or age
GENOCIDES	when a lot of people are killed that belong to a certain group, usually to do with race or country
HERITAGE	something that is inherited from earlier generations such as traits, language, buildings, etc.
IDENTIFIES	to feel linked to something, or to feel that it describes you
INDIGENOUS	originating or naturally found in a particular place
INHERITED	passed down from a parent
INSTITUTIONAL RACISM	racial discrimination that has become the normal behaviour of an organisation
MINORITIES	a group that differs in race, ethnic background or culture to the majority of a population
NOMADIC	not living in one permanent place
ORGANISATIONS	organised groups of people who work together for a shared purpose
PHYSICAL	relating to the body
POLICE BRUTALITY	when a member of the police uses more force than necessary to uphold the law
PREJUDICE	an opinion, judgement, or belief that is formed without knowing the facts
REPRESENTATION	when someone, or a group of people, are represented by someone speaking or acting on their behalf
RIOTS	noisy, violent and uncontrolled public reactions
SEGREGATION	the act of separating groups of people
SELF-ESTEEM	how someone feels about themselves and their own ability
SUPREMACISTS	a group of people who promote the idea that one group or race is better than all others
TRAITS	qualities or characteristics of a person

INDEX

A
aboriginal 26–27
apartheid 18, 28

B
Barack Obama 20, 23
bullying 8, 12

C
charities 25, 28, 30
culture 5, 9, 11, 16–17, 23, 26–27, 29

D
depression 14
difference 4–7, 9, 17, 20
discrimination 6–9, 11, 22, 27–28
diversity 23

E
education 11, 17, 25, 27, 30
equality 9, 20, 23–25, 28

F
friends 10, 15, 25

H
heritage 4–5, 13

I
identity 4–5

M
Martin Luther King Jr. 19, 28
media 12, 19, 22
microaggressions 13
minorities 21

N
Nelson Mandela 18, 28

P
police 8, 19, 21–22
prejudice 6–8, 10, 17
protests 19, 21

R
representation 20, 22–23, 28
riots 15, 19, 21

S
segregation 18–19
stereotypes 6, 17, 28

W
WWII 18